MANIPULATION

A Beginner's Guide to Learn and Perfect the Art of Manipulation

NEAL D. ROSCHMANN

Table of Contents

Introduction

I want to thank you and congratulate you for downloading the book, *Manipulation: Beginners Guide to Learn and Perfect the Art of Manipulation.*

This book contains tried-and-tested beginner level techniques and strategies on how to get people to do what you want them to using the power of influence, persuasion, communication skills, and manipulation.

The book is a comprehensive beginner manipulation handbook that is packed with lots of little-known manipulation strategies, secrets of mind control, and actionable techniques that can be implemented right away for influencing and manipulating people.

From talking your way into a promotion with your manager to asking someone you've only just met out for a date, there's just no stopping where and how you can use this priceless information contained in the power-packed beginner's manipulation resource. I've provided lots of everyday examples and illustrations to make the understanding simpler and more engaging.

Thanks again for downloading this book. I hope you'll enjoy it!

Chapter 1:
Manipulation Demystified

Even before we understood the term manipulation, or the psychological concept of manipulation came into being, we've been manipulating and getting manipulated. As newborns, we manipulated our caregivers into feeding, keeping us clean and putting us to sleep. As infants, we manipulated adults for toys and treats. As adolescents, we manipulated our parents/caregivers for permission for late nights.

Again, as professionals, we manipulate our employers into hiking our pay or promoting us. We try to manipulate people on a daily basis in big and small ways. For example, you may persuade a coworker to fill in for you when you are away on vacation even when he/she has plenty of his/her own stuff to do. Gosh, didn't I manipulate you into downloading this book too?

The truth is knowingly or unknowingly, we are all part of the giving or receiving end of manipulation. We resort to several techniques to get others to do precisely what we want them to, sometimes even harming them in the process.

Fundamentally, manipulation is the art of getting people to do what you desire by using clever (often sneaky and cunning) techniques including charm, persuasion, coxing, lying, hypnotism, charisma, and more. While influence and persuasion have largely positive connotations, manipulation has more sinister undertones. It is seen as a negative persuasion tactic used for exploiting people to serve one's purposes.

Manipulation often operates from the perspective of, "I have to trick people to accomplish my goal." Having said that, not all manipulation types are bad! Depending on how you use it, it can also be used to serve a positive means. Sometimes, you may use a negative technique to serve a positive goal, which doesn't make manipulation so bad after all.

Let's say, for example, that you've been working really hard in your current organization. You've brought your employer's plenty of business and goodwill. However, they are depriving you of the salary raise and promotion that is long since due. Each time you ask for it, they come up with a clever excuse.

In such a scenario, if you manipulate your way into claiming what is rightfully yours, you aren't so wrong. You may threaten to leave and join another company, take away their clients by forming a company of your own or influence other employees to move to companies where their skills are more valued. You are using manipulation to accomplish a positive goal.

Manipulation primarily originates from the idea that your desires, goals, and needs are above everyone. You alone at the focal point of the universe and everything should revolve around your wishes and needs. Manipulators take advantage of other people's feelings and emotions to fulfill their needs. You can lend it a less evil twist by aligning it with the desire for the greater good or a win-win, where everyone benefits. Again, it can be used in a positive manner if you get people to do what is beneficial for them by manipulating their thoughts and actions. This way, the person doesn't think they are being tricked or pushed into doing something that goes against their interests.

For example, you love a person deeply and know that you are capable of keeping them happy and cared for throughout your life. You will convince him/her to marry you and spend the rest of their life with you. This is a positive manipulation or influence, where the other person doesn't end up feeling he/she is being exploited. Through manipulation, you are accomplishing a goal that is beneficial for both—you and them. Is it so bad in such a scenario? You are trying to persuade the person into a loving and powerful bond that you firmly believe in.

Think of manipulation as a hammer (or any other tool) that can be handily used to fix a nail in the wall or for destroying a work of art. Manipulation is a tool that can be used either to achieve a positive/constructive outcome or to destroy a person's sense of self-worth or feelings. It can be positive or negative depending on your intentions and the goal used to achieve it.

The manipulation tool is in your hand—you decide how to use it.

Have you watched any of Shakespeare's tragedies like Othello or Macbeth?

The ingenious playwright comprehended manipulation even before the term probably existed. The plots of Shakespeare's tragedies almost always revolve around manipulation. For example, Lady Macbeth manipulates her husband through multiple psychological techniques into murdering King Duncan and overtaking the Scottish throne. Later, he goes into a maniacal killing spree to protect himself from enmity. The aftermath is a bloodbath, which leads to the death of Macbeth and his wife.

Lady Macbeth and the evil witch siblings use manipulation throughout the story. They use sneaky tricks to persuade Lord Macbeth into performing horrifying acts that lead to his eventual downfall. They plant the seed of insidious ambition that he alone deserves to be the ruler, thus making Macbeth hate Duncan, which leads him to murder Duncan.

Another Shakespeare tragedy that has manipulation as its central theme is Othello. Lago, the tricky and ambitious villain, plots to sow the seeds of suspicion in the eyes of Othello against the latter's ladylove Desdemona. Lago wants Cassio (who is Othello's most trusted aide) out of the picture to take over the chief lieutenant's place. Through a series of cleverly crafted tricks and manipulative scenarios, he convinces Othello to believe that Cassio is being disloyal to him by being romantically involved with the master Othello's love Desdemona. He constructs a series of events that inject doubt, betrayal, and hatred in Othello's mind, which leads to him killing his ladylove. Thus, an orchestration of circumstances, words, and actions help Lago eliminate Cassio from his way and take over the position of Othello's main lieutenant. Thus, deception and sinister manipulative techniques have been a part of literature even before the fancy terms for it came into being.

This is exactly what manipulation is all about. However, despite the fact that manipulation has low-brow connotations, manipulation is not always bad. It can be channelized positively to accomplish a greater good. It can be utilized for triggering positive change, which wouldn't be possible using regular persuasion and influence techniques.

Irrespective of whether you realize or not, you are being perpetually influenced by people to act in a manner that is beneficial to them. Think about how advertisements or marketers manipulate you into buying something you may not even need.

You begin to desire or want something you don't really need because as a consumer, you are being led to think in a particular way. For example, "only abc shoes make you look like a cool, expert and professional athlete." Naturally, every athlete wants to look expert and cool, so you end up buying a pair of shoes you don't really need.

Similarly, a political party may urge you to vote for them if you want things to change. Of course, we all want to progress and change and thus end up voting for the party who is looking to fulfill their agenda of rising to power. There is really no escaping from manipulation in our daily lives.

Is Positive Manipulation a Reality?

Yes, manipulation can be utilized in a constructive manner to transform a negative sentiment into a positive experience through the physical, mental, and spiritual aspects of your personality. It can be used to help someone get rid of an addiction or a disorder. Imagine the power of getting an addict to release themselves from the clutches of drug addiction or getting a binge eater to adopt healthier eating patterns.

You are using positive manipulation to make someone to do what is in their best interests. History has several examples of positive manipulation bringing about the desired effect. The world's greatest leaders and religious evangelists, including Martin Luther King, Mahatma Gandhi, Gautama Buddha, and Jesus Christ, influenced people and pulled them into their ideologies like magnets. They spread across a positive energy that spoke of justice, brotherhood, and equality. That wouldn't qualify as an evil manipulation, would it? These leaders spread an intensely constructive vibe via their words, actions, and life to guide others on a similar path of humanity.

These figures didn't use manipulation in a negative sense. They used the power of influence and persuasion to help people learn important life lessons.

Just consider this scenario for a moment. There are several situations in life where you feel an urge to reach out to someone who needs your help. For example, your sibling is keeping bad company, and you feel a compelling urge to get him or her out of this destructive peer group. None of the straight or seemingly positive ways you've used has helped you remove them from the clutches of negative influence. In such a scenario, is manipulation bad? If you sue the underhand tactics to help people do what is good for them, is manipulation an evil concept?

The motive or intention behind the act of manipulation makes all the difference. The motives here are hardly selfish or self-serving. The techniques may be a little sneakily or crafty, but that intention or purpose doesn't make it so bad after all.

Haven't you heard how desperate times call for desperate measures? Sometimes, you have to use the back-door or underhand techniques when convincing people in a straightforward manner isn't possible. You may have tried everything you can within reasonable influence and persuasion tactics. However, when nothing else works, one often resorts to what is viewed as crafty measures.

Watch out for the intent with which you are manipulating people. If it is for sales or to help someone act in a manner that is positive and beneficial for them, manipulation may not be as evil as it is portrayed to be. However, if you trample on other people's sense of self-worth, emotions, well-being, or fundamental rights to serve your needs, the manipulation gets downright evil.

MANIPULATION

If you are using manipulation to overcome the obstinacy, irrationality, or stubbornness, it may be a negative means for a positive cause.

Let us consider an example to understand this more effectively.

Your best friend (let's call him Tim) is someone you deeply care about. You've been thick since childhood, having shared the same neighborhood, values, and school. A mutual friend lets you know that Tim (who has now moved to another city for work) has been abandoned by his long-time girlfriend for another man just days before they were to get married. The depression has caused his performance to deteriorate at work.

You know being a sensitive and emotional person; Tim must be hurting from within. The incident has taken a toll on his personal and professional life. You go over to meet him and suggest that he'll see a counselor before his feelings get worse. He simply refuses to accept that there is a problem and is not open to seeing a counselor. However hard you try to persuade, please, or coerce him, it doesn't work.

What's the next move for going past his obstinacy?

As a friend, you are terribly concerned about Tim. However, reasonable persuasion doesn't seem to be working with him.

In desperation, you tell him about how your manager's son met with a near-fatal accident and slipped into a coma. The manager went into a bout of depression, following which his performance at work was disturbed. You choose the right words, expressions, emotions, and voice tone to convey your idea. The narrative is slowly built to the point where the manager is about to lose his job and destroy his personal and professional life.

This is when you tell Tim how the manager agreed to seek professional help to bring his life back on track. You booked an appointment for your manager, and on your suggestion, he started going for a regular therapy/counseling. Masterfully, you inform Tim how with a strong will and a series of counseling sessions combined with therapy helped the manager regain control of his life. You are attempting to stir the right emotions in Tim to get him to take action in the right direction. There's hope that he will be sufficiently moved into action after hearing the account of your manager.

Not one word of what you spoke is true. It is lies and deception! You just made it all up to get Tim to take action. You manipulated Tim into meeting a therapist so that he could take control of his life again. The motive was to improve his psychological condition through a little trickery and deception. Manipulation opens a little window to surpass an individual's defenses or obstinacy to get them to act in a more positive direction.

The following are some ways that qualify as manipulation:

- Constant complaining
- Being a helpless victim
- Inducing a feeling of guilt
- Comparing the victim with others
- Giving excuses, justifications, and rationalizing
- Pretending ignorance

- Emotional blackmail
- Acting evasive
- Showing fake concern
- Putting down people
- Constantly blaming others for their troubles
- Lying and trickery
- Denying
- Fake flattery
- Intimidation
- Offering an illusion of selflessness
- Shaming victims

The Psychology of Manipulation and Influencing People

Manipulation as a tool can be used to influence or persuade people in a negative or positive manner depending on the intent. Robert B. Cialdini, a social psychologist, gave six major influences that, when mastered, allow an individual to influence other people's thoughts, words, and actions.

Again, these techniques can be used in a positive or negative manner. You are holding a matchstick that can be utilized for lighting either a flame or a disastrous fire. How you use the potent tool of manipulation and influence is up to you.

1. Social Proof

Since primitive times, man has the tendency to follow the herd. People believe that if everyone else is doing something, it must be good or the right way to do something. Fashion and trends are nothing but a result of people following other people who set trends. One of the most powerful ways to influence people is to offer social proof because it doesn't make them come across as they isolated in their decisions and actions.

For example, when you are called for a party, don't we all have the tendency to ask who else will be attending it? Don't you feel more persuaded to attend when you realize that everyone else from your friends' circle or social group will be in attendance? The fear or insecurity of being left out makes people take quick decisions. Therefore, social proof is a huge influence, persuasion, and manipulation tool.

2. Authority

Notice how all the health and wellness advertisements or promotions have doctors or health experts speaking about how consumers will benefit from these products or services. Social media influencers thrive on influencing people through building their authority credibility and expertise. They like to position themselves as experts who can guide people with the right knowledge.

Authority is an individual who is looked up to by others for advice, suggestions, or recommendations in a certain field. If you want to influence and persuade, bring in a person who is seen to be in an authoritative position.

Introduce a person in a position of authority if you want someone to do something your way. If I urge you to buy a fashion label, you may not. However, if Rihanna or Kim Kardashian urges you to buy the same label, you may give it a thought. Authority works powerfully when it comes to influencing people. An expert can convince people in the way regular folks may not be able to.

3. Reciprocity

When someone does you a favor, you subconsciously feel obliged to return it. You feel you owe the person something until you return it. It gives the other person the upper hand over you. For example, if a friend gives you an expensive present, you feel compelled to do something equally huge in return.

If you want to get people to do things your way, make them feel obliged towards you by doing them a favor. I know a lot of people who when you thank them, come back with, "Oh! It's nothing really, wouldn't you do the same for me?" instead of "It isn't really a big deal, please don't mention it." By saying the former, they are simply trying to make you feel obliged into doing something for them in the future. So, if you want someone to do something for you in the future, get them to feel obliged.

4. Scarcity

Since primitive times, it is a tendency for us as humans to value things that are perceived as scarce or rarely available. This is the psychology sales and marketing professionals use on their buyers by stating "limited edition," "until stocks last," "last few left," "exclusive offer," and much more. It is a human tendency to grab what is seen as limited. If you want to persuade, influence, or manipulate someone into thinking or acting in a specific way, get them to think something is limited, scarce, rare, or exclusive.

5. Attractiveness

Honestly, wouldn't you be more taken in by an attractive-looking salesperson trying to sell you something over a plain-looking salesperson selling you the exact same thing. There are an appeal, a charisma, and a magnetic charm that attractive people radiate that helps them persuade people more easily. However, much we deny, we are taken in by the friendly, physically attractive, and charming folks. Spending time with people to get them familiar to you is a great way of building rapport or influencing people.

For example, if you want to ask a person out on a date, rather than asking them out straight off, hang out with them as friends. This way, you have a higher chance of getting them to agree on a date. There are less likely to say no because of the familiarity factor. Manipulating and persuading people become easier when you establish familiarity. Wouldn't it be difficult for you to refuse people you know over people who are absolute strangers?

6. Commitment

When you manage to lock someone into a commitment, it is simpler to get them to do it. For example, if a person gives something in writing, they will be likelier to do it owing to accountability. There is an inherent fear of being held responsible for committing to something. If you want someone to do something specific for you, get them to commit to it in front of other people, in writing, or in a public platform. It will tougher for them to backtrack if they announce their decision publicly.

Chapter 2:
Brilliant Psychological Techniques for Manipulating and Influence People

We manipulate people and get manipulated on a daily basis, though the intention and intensity keep varying. There are plenty of tricks to get people to do what you want them to.

How can you get people to do what you want them to each time? What are some of the most tried-and-tested influence and persuasion strategies that help you exercise control over people's words, thoughts, actions, and emotions?

Here are some of the most effective manipulation strategies that will help you to have your way with people.

1. Setting Similarity

Establishing similarity is a powerful way to get people to do things your way. This works for everything from asking your manager for a promotion to getting the hot new girl/boy agree for a date. This works on a very primordial level. Since primitive times, people take to people who are like them or they perceive to be one among them. There is a subconscious feeling of affiliation towards people we perceive to be like us. When we get people to think we are "like me," they are likelier to do what you want them to.

The next time you want to manipulate or influence people, mirror their actions. Observe how they walk, talk, words they use, their actions, gestures, and expressions. Subtly mirror their body language, including gestures and posture. For example, observe how a person is holding their glass of drink and follow suit. Sip your drink right after they do, or gesticulate like them, or lean against the bar like them. If you notice the person moving their weight from one foot to another, mirror their action.

There is a deep psychological process behind the act of mirroring. When you mirror a person's words and actions, you are simply reinforcing the fact that you are one among them. Make the mirroring subtler, it shouldn't come across as you are imitating or mimicking a person. If the mirroring becomes too obvious, the person is likelier to get offended. This may have a negative impact on your intent of getting the person to do what you want them to.

The method is effective when you are getting someone to agree with your point in negotiations or a professional set-up, where emotions don't work.

2. Build Charisma

You can't explain charisma. It's either there or not. Though charisma cannot be explained, it can be easily identified in people. Most politicians, world leaders, performers, and salespersons consciously work on their charisma to make the process of getting others to do what they want smoother. They work on their charm effortlessly and hypnotize people with their words and actions to behave in a certain way. Do you spread a friendly and warm vibe? Do you have a friendly, open and positive language? Can you win people over with a gripping conversation even when you are meeting them for the first time? Can you sweep people off their feet by creating a dazzling first impression?

People adept in the art of persuasion have well-developed conversation skills. They have a gift of the gab (smooth talkers) that can make other people feel special. Manipulators have a knack for using body language to their advantage. Through your words and actions, make people feel like you are genuinely listening to them.

Give them the impression that you care about their feelings and interests. Show them that you care enough to make an effort to get to know them, even when you don't.

Confidence is one of the biggest charisma enhancers. Confident and self-assured people are hugely charismatic. When you know exactly what you are doing or saying, your confidence is reassuring for people. They realize you know your stuff. When you have complete faith in your abilities, it becomes easier to influence, persuade, or manipulate people to act in a manner that is beneficial for you.

When people are confident in their abilities, words, or actions, they can easily inspire others. For example, imagine dealing with a salesperson who doesn't know what he or she is saying about the product. They are unsure about the product features or unable to answer your questions about it convincingly. Will they inspire you to purchase the product? No, right? As a buyer, you'll think that if they themselves aren't convinced about their product, how on earth they expect you to be sure of it!

People will take your words and actions seriously when they are assured that you know precisely what you are saying or doing. This comes with practiced confidence and communication skills (more on developing the manipulator communication skills later). Irrespective of whether you are speaking the truth or not, you need to say it in a confident and impactful manner to drive the other person into taking the required action.

3. Compare and Contrast Technique

This is another clever manipulation technique that each of us has used knowingly or unknowingly at some point. It is effective owing to the human psychological element it attempts to play on. There's nothing fancy about it yet, but it works a majority of the times based on a simple principle.

You make an unreasonable request first and then follow it up with a more practical or reasonable request (this is what you want, the manipulator to actually do). What you end up doing is offering the other person an opportunity to weigh the first unreasonable request against the second reasonable one, where the second request comes across as really small and doable.

They will be a bit shaken or thrown off the balance with the initial request and then feel psychologically comforted by the second request. This whirlwind of emotions can support brilliantly in favor of the manipulator.

Let us say, for instance, if you want a day's leave in the middle of a hectic project, you ask your manager for 15 day's leave to visit your parents. He/she will most likely scream at you for even coming up with such an unreasonable request smack in the middle of an important project.

However, you feign disappointment and quickly follow it up (the key is not waste any more time) with a more reasonable request such as a day off from work, which will compensate for by working extra hours during the rest of the week. This sounds way more reasonable compared to the initial request, and your boss is likelier to be relieved in this request. Thus, he'll end up saying yes to a day's leave (that you thought was almost impossible in the beginning). Once a person says "no" to you, it becomes more challenging to follow it up with another "no," especially if the later request is smaller compared to the first.

4. Be the Victim

This classic manipulation technique involves playing the victim. Think carefully about how a certain section of people will use the victim card cleverly for social and political benefits. They will present themselves as marginalized and disadvantaged to gain support.

They will stir the popular opinion their way by manipulating people into thinking they've been victims. They will use the unfairness and demonstrate (belonging to a specific race, ethnicity, religion, etc.) to their advantage. Using this tactic, they try to cash in on their helplessness. Ensure that you don't overdo it since it can backfire if pushed too aggressively.

Basically, you are informing others about how everyone and everything has gone against your interest to gain something. Sounding like everyone is conspiring against you makes you come across as a hapless victim and attracts sympathy your way.

Several manipulators use this technique to get the mileage they seek rather than fighting. They will act calm and accept the situation.

5. Present Your Interests as Altruism

Pretend to have the other person's interests in mind even though your interests are paramount. This is a great manipulation tactic to get people to do what you want them to. If you openly criticize people or scream them for not doing something, they may get defensive. However, if you present in a manner that you genuinely have the person's interest in mind, he/she will be likelier to be influenced by what you say. Cover your criticism or interests as altruism. Your image should be that of a person who is concerned enough to reach out and help others.

Explain to people how you are acting purely on their interests, which is playing on your mind. Rationalize the reason for your outburst and criticism by putting it across like you care for them. Inquire what can be done to make the task easier? Pledge help and support when it comes to always being around for them. People will invariably shed their defenses and be more open to doing what you want them to if you portray it as being beneficial for them or being concerned about them.

Psychologically, people are most vulnerable just after making a mistake. They think people will be against them or hold them accountable for their mistakes. This makes them more defensive. Rather than criticizing people, project yourself as an altruistic that is keen on helping them. People will quickly buy what you say.

6. Bribery

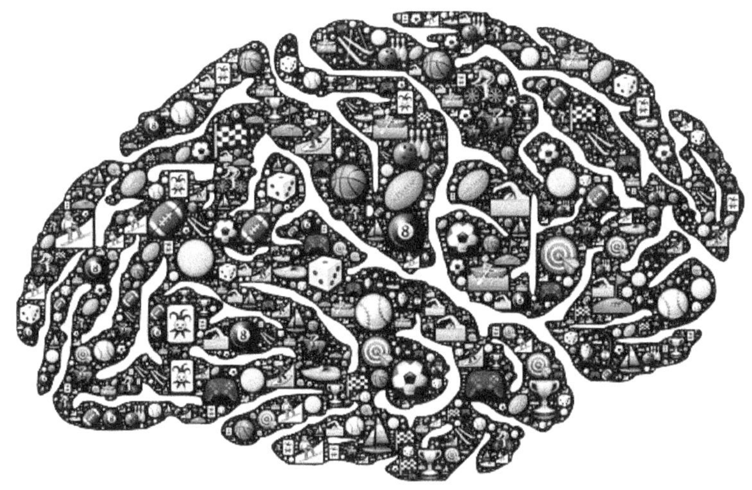

This is another clever technique that is highly effective when it comes to getting people to do what you want them to in personal, social, or professional settings. Give people psychological rewards and make them feel obliged to return the favor. Ensure that when they do give back the favor, you use it to your advantage.

Recognize people's wants and give them exactly what they want. Subtly, establish that you are going beyond your capacity of the call of duty to do them a favor. Also, mention that when you need help, they should also be prepared to go out of the way. When it is, strike back with your request. They will feel compelled to oblige.

Don't portray this as an exchange or blackmail, which can backfire. Present it in the angle that you are approaching the person genuinely and trying to help them. This tactic is effective because people view a clear benefit and, therefore, feel more influenced by doing something.

For example, if you are filling in for a coworker, ensure that your manager is well aware that you are going out of the way to complete your coworker's task by staying late and working for a few hours over the weekend. Follow this up by asking your manager for a few days off in the next week. It is almost impossible for them to refuse your request.

7. Make the Victim Feel Guilty

Guilt is a powerful way to manipulate people into doing what you want them to. This works effectively especially on people who are filled with self-doubt or are low on self-confidence/self-esteem. Manipulators generally use this technique on people who are indecisive or vulnerable by nature.

Let us say, for instance, a teenager wants to go on an overnight weekend trip with friends. He/she knows that they will most likely get a no for an answer if they ask in a straightforward manner. Thereafter begins the game of guilt. They'll make their parents feel guilty about the fact that they've been overprotective or haven't allowed them to explore or negotiate the world on their own.

How will they learn to navigate the world on their own if they don't step outside the house or make their own decisions or practice living by themselves? They explain how they haven't got an opportunity to live life on their terms. All of this induces a sense of guilt and can make the parents give in to their demands.

Similarly, if you want to get a friend or spouse to do something, list the things you've done for them and how they've been unfair to you on several occasions. Say something like, "I couldn't expect anything better from me. It is my fault that I thought you'd do this for me." It is like inducing guilt through emotional blackmail.

Notice how some parents manipulate their children by telling them they don't have time for their parents or they don't do much for their parents. They will speak about how short their life is and how they've brought up their children with care, and that the children don't reciprocate owing to their busy schedules. This is also a subtle form of emotional manipulation.

Guilt is a powerful manipulation factor. It makes the victim feel emotionally bound to the manipulator and do things the way he/she wants them to.

8. Play on the Fear-Relief Cycle

This is used by almost every marketer, advertiser, promoter, and salesperson to market or sell his products/services. They will get you to take the desired action (buying their product or service) by sowing seeds of the worst that can happen in a situation. This will be followed by presenting their product/service as the solution.

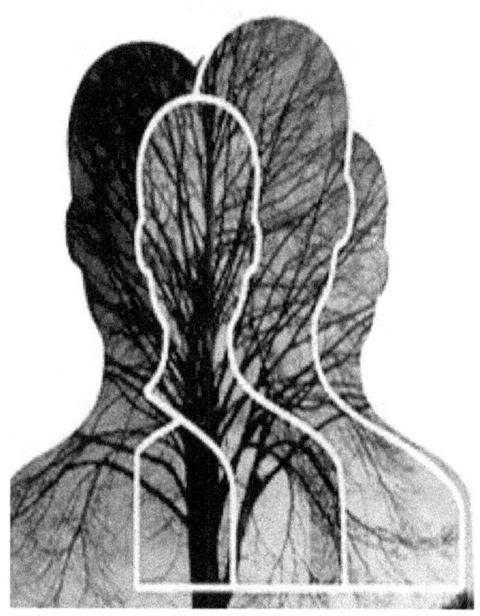

This strategy makes the victim go through a cycle of emotions. The fear will get them nervous, followed by the solution that attempts to bring instant relief and hope.

For instance, the life insurance advertisements always play on the fear of what will happen to your loved ones after you pass away. They create a sense of fear and panic, followed by a seemingly simple solution of buying a policy that ensures your loved ones don't fall short of money to cater to their needs and fulfill their dreams. The sneaky trick instills a sense of hope and relief and drives you to take action (purchase the policy).

Another example is "When I borrowed your camera for the prom night, I really thought I heard something snap inside it. I was damn sure I broke something inside the camera. However, I looked back and realized it was a guy watching a tech video on his phone. Wasn't that funny? Oh, and may I borrow your camera again for a weekend birthday party if you are alright with it?"

Again, you are taking the person through a cycle where you are inducing fear and then offering them relief by stating that it wasn't as bad as what you said earlier. This puts them in a more positive state of mind, where they are likelier to agree with you.

Notice how when children want to communicate their less-than-flattering grades to their parents will end up saying something like they flunked the subject. When the parent gets really upset, they'll come back with, "Relax it's not so bad, I just got a C." The parent doesn't feel so bad after all!

9. Flirt

Flirting is another powerful manipulation tactic that can be brilliantly leveraged to get people to do as you desire. Aren't we guilty of resorting to flirting at some point to get the other person to do something for us? You can't coerce people to do what you want them to all the time. They should like you to agree to your request/demand. When people like or adore you, it is easier to get them to act as per your whims and fancies. It's like casting a hypnotic or enchanting spell on them to win them over.

Once you win a person over, it becomes easy to get them to do what you want. You are creating a bunch of positive emotions in their mind towards you. You are gaining power over their thoughts and feelings by making a positive impression on them.

The idea is to flirt in a more gentle, subtle and positive manner by getting rid of your differences and inhibitions. Use a couple of positive expressions or touches rather than going completely overboard (and, in turn, scaring the person away). It can be a light or subtle tap on the person's arm or the back of their palm. Ruffling their hair or leaning slightly more than normal in another person's direction is another effective flirting tactic.

Avoid being disrespectful or aggressive when someone doesn't take too well to your flirtatious ways. Respect their personal space and boundaries even while trying to manipulate them into doing what you want. People don't take too kindly to being pushed around. Flirting is all about adding charm to the communication or coming across as a charming person. If a person feels like you are intruding their private space, you'll come across as anything but charming. Flirting as a manipulation tool works wonderfully well on people who have low self-esteem or low self-worth. When you make such a person feel wonderful about themselves by flirting, you almost always win their vote.

10. Study a Master Manipulator

There is no better way you master the dynamics of manipulation than from observing an expert manipulator closely. It can be anyone from a friend to your sales manager to a family member to a nemesis who is adept in the art of manipulation. Study this person closely and take valuable notes. Notice carefully how this person always has his or her way. This will offer you fresh insights and manipulation ideas.

11. Know When to Turn the Tables

If a person you are using manipulation techniques on accuses you of manipulating them or calls out to your manipulative technique, don't admit to it. Rather, look genuinely shocked, upset, or hurt. Pretend to be shattered and say something to the effect of, "I just can't believe you said that" or "I wouldn't in my wildest dreams imagine you can think something like this." You have to make the other person feel even sadder and guiltier than before for suggesting something like this.

Understand that if you admit to using manipulation to have your way, it will be challenging to get the person to do something for you in the future.

Chapter 3:
Social Manipulation Strategies

Here are some of the most powerful strategies for manipulating people in the social or public settings and scenarios.

1. Cash in on the Home Court

Ever noticed why several network marketing professionals always insist that you come to their home or office for a presentation rather than giving you a presentation in your home? There is a simple manipulation strategy behind it. When you negotiate within a physical space that belongs to you, subconsciously you are in a more authoritative position.

This is one of the biggest social manipulation secrets that few will tell you about. You have greater influence, control, power, and dominance when you are in a physical space that is your domain. It reflects in your body language, attitude, words, and actions. The place can be anywhere from your home to office to car, which you are comfortable and familiar with. Network marketers are always attempting to cash in on the home court advantage, which is why they will insist that you come over for a presentation to their place.

When you are signing an important deal or negotiating terms of a critical association, always persuade the other party into coming over to your office or home for a talk. The comfort and familiarity of your space will put you in a position of greater confidence and authority, thus increasing your chances of cracking the deal in your favor.

Tell people that they need to understand the process or you need to explain everything to them in detail, which is why they should come over to your place. This is the angle you present to them. The reality is that you are giving yourself a higher position by conducting negotiations in a space that you own and are therefore familiar and comfortable in.

2. Distraction Strategy

This is one of the most common manipulation techniques used by governments, political parties, world leaders, politicians, and other public personalities to divert the public attention from the vital problems by introducing continuous distractions and trivial/unimportant information.

This way, the public attention remains fixated on insignificant issues while the true political and social issues are hidden under the carpet. It gives the public the illusion of being busy with something, though that something is of little consequence in their life. They don't have the time to think about the negative impact of important issues in their life and the inability of their leaders to resolve these issues.

3. Create Problems That Don't Exist and Offer Solutions

This is another classic social manipulation strategy that is widely used throughout the world. It consists of creating an imaginary or foreseen issue to stimulate a specific reaction among victims of manipulation or the public. Then, the manipulator carefully introduces a solution to become the ultimate messiah.

For example, allowing urban violence to build and thrive initially or supporting terrorist camps. This can be followed by making people aware of how their security is the government's prime concern and how leaders will go all out to intensify security measures to ensure the public safety.

You introduce a problem and then offer a solution for the problem without letting the victims realize that you were directly responsible for creating the problems. This way, you become the solution provider, who can get people to act in a desired manner.

4. The Painful Reality

Let us consider a scenario to understand this strategy clearly. Your boss urges everyone at the workplace to put in additional hours of work or work during weekends. He/she may lead you to believe that you all stand to lose your jobs and the market is really tight, which means that you have to step up and go the extra mile to survive. They will inform you about how other companies who weren't able to bag big projects couldn't sustain operation costs and eventually closed down.

The managers will convince you about how a few sacrifices from your side can go a long way in saving the company's fortunes. You see what they are doing there? They are projecting their decision as painful yet necessary. They'll tell how they don't really want you to stay late at work, but there's no other option if you want to keep your job or the company has to stay afloat.

A majority will resign to the idea of working late.

5. To Project Victims as Ignorant or Stupid

The easiest way to get people to do what you want them to do publicly, professionally, or socially is to make them feel how ignorant or stupid they or how they don't understand something. For instance, if you are looking to introduce new technology that will save labor costs and increase profits, it may have a bunch of people rebelling against it for fear of losing their jobs.

By using the ignorant manipulation tactic, you inform people about how they do not have the capacity to comprehend technology, which is designed to make things easier. Basically, you are playing on their lack of awareness or uncertainty about a thing. You are telling them that they aren't in a position to give their view or opinion about it because they do not have the right knowledge or understanding about these systems.

Again, you are replacing revolt with guilt by making the victims feel like they themselves are responsible for their unfortunate situation or their lack of intelligence /capabilities. Thus, instead of rebelling, workers blame or devaluate themselves, thus inhibiting further action.

6. Foot in the Door Strategy

This technique dates back to the times of door-to-door salespersons (hence, the name). To prevent people from shutting their doors on their face, the salespersons use to put their foot in the door and request a couple of minutes to speak to the homeowners.

Once they got those 2-3 minutes with the homeowners, they would build upon it and try to sell their products to them.

Thus, in a social or public setting, this is one of the most effective manipulation techniques because it gives you that tiny opening, which you can cleverly encase on. You attempt to break the ice by making a small request from the other person that they generally won't refuse. This is followed by the actual or bigger request. What you are doing by asking for a smaller request to be fulfilled in putting you gently in the door and triggering a series of positive replies.

Once a person agrees to a small request, it is more challenging to follow it with a refusal. The trick here is to request for something tiny and reasonable that the victim can easily fulfill. This is to be followed by the actual intended or larger request.

7. Drown Them with Facts, Information, and Statistics

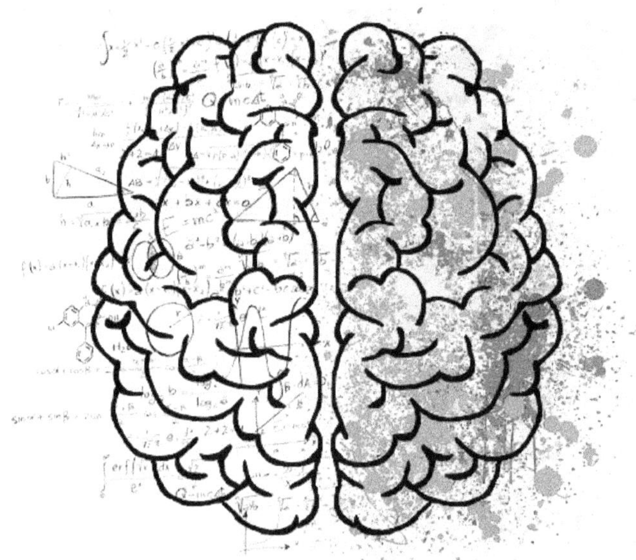

Emotional manipulation doesn't work on everyone, especially in the social and professional settings. Here, people are more inclined to follow the logic and rational arguments. Drown these folks in information by quoting research, facts, figures, statistics, and more.

Have numbers ready on your fingertips for any objections and clarifications. Overwhelm people with statistics, logical arguments, and research. Be armed with the vital information to "intellectually bully" people. Present yourself as the ultimate authority or the source of knowledge in a particular field. Cleverly present research that supports your stand or point of view. Take advantage of an established expertise to the fullest.

One of the best ways to manipulate people with logic is to present research, statistics, and figures in a compelling and imposing manner. Focus on areas where you believe they may not have sound knowledge and question them about it. This establishes their weakness in their own eyes. They will realize that they have little or no information about this area and that you are more experienced or knowledgeable than them.

This will automatically increase your chances of getting them to do what you want them to. This technique works well during business negotiations, sales, social debates, and other social or public settings.

You gain a smart subconscious edge over the other person, which makes them more defenseless and open to listening to you. It creates a sort of intellectual superiority, which makes them feel inadequate and compels them to comply with your demands.

8. The Victim Talks First

When you are getting another party to agree to your negotiation terms or buy from you, allow them to talk first. This gives you an opportunity as a persuader, influencer, or manipulator to establish their baseline. What are their strengths and weaknesses? What are their thoughts, emotions, fears, and behavior patterns? Are they more hesitant or self-confident? Do they appear extroverted/open or introverted/closed? Are they approaching the deal or sales with an element of hesitation? Are they overwhelmed by your presence? How does their body language reveal about them?

Allowing them to communicate first helps you set a baseline for both their strengths and weaknesses, which can be utilized to get them to act in the desired direction. You can also prepare a list of questions that you can ask them to establish a baseline. The idea is to get them thinking in the direction of taking action in your favor. For instance, if you are planning to sell insurance, you ask them a list of questions that help you establish their fears and therefore give you to the opportunity to play on these fears for getting them to sign up quickly.

9. Kill Trust Issues by Sharing Something Personal

A lot of people are wary of being manipulated because they've been misled or manipulated in the past. They come with a baggage of trust issues and always operate with a hint of suspicion. Such people are potentially difficult to manipulate since they always have their guard on.

However, one way to overcome trust issues or help them drop their guard is by sharing personal information. This makes them lower the walls and increase their trust in you. Ensure that the information you share is confidential or personal enough to break the trust barrier. Share something that they can relate to or is important for them to know to make the strategy even more effective. The information you share may be real or fabricated. However, it is important that the other person believes it.

10. Be a Master at Debates and Public Speaking

Like we discussed in the previous chapter, manipulation is all about building charisma. It is about being able to persuade or influence people into taking the desired action. If you want to develop your persuasion or people-convincing skills, sign up for a public speaking class. You will learn to put across your point in a gripping, impactful and assertive manner without getting aggressive or pushy.

Notice how some of the best public speakers or orators can hypnotically charm people with their verbal and nonverbal communication skills. They use everything from their words to gestures to posture to voice tone to persuade people into thinking or acting like them. Convincing people takes a confident and powerful persona.

When you portray a confident and imposing personality, people automatically sit up and pay attention to what you are saying. Attract people like magnets by learning the powerful strategies for appearing more convincing and presenting ideas in a more attention-grabbing/spellbinding manner.

To enhance your theatrics and/or communication skills, sign up for a theater or drama workshop. One of the greatest challenges in manipulating people is not just controlling your emotions and expressions but also having complete control over your body language, gestures, and expressions to portray the desired feelings or emotions. If you don't want to sign up for an acting class or theater workshop, study the mannerisms of actors. Examine the way actors express emotions.

Notice how they use the tone of their voice to create the desired impact. Observe how they pause at the right places to allow the significance of what they said to sink in. This should give you a good idea of skills you need to develop as a master manipulator or persuader.

So, you may be really happy that the person is about to do what you want them to. Yet, you may have to portray a different emotion to control the emotion of elation. Manipulating speech, expressions, gesture, posture, the tone of voice, and other similar verbal and nonverbal communication patterns require practice.

Contriving emotions becomes easy when you can complement them with matching nonverbal clues. For example, have you practiced looking dejected and hurt when you don't get what you want? How about faking certain emotions when you clearly don't feel them?

Signing up for a drama, acting, or theater workshop makes you adept in honing your speech and acting histrionics, which are vital for boosting manipulation or persuasion powers. Haven't you observed how salespersons resort to extreme histrionics when they want to get you to buy something? Their body language, gestures, and expressions are amusingly exaggerated.

One of the biggest qualities of a master manipulator is that they have total control over their emotions. They don't allow their emotions to rule them. Actively practice controlling your emotions if you want to manipulate or influence people successfully. At times, people influencers or persuaders have to shed tears at the drop of a hat or laugh according to the situation. You will have to build a variety of emotions or expressions, which is a vital skill from the manipulation perspective.

11. Tweak the Environment to Gain Advantage

You can use the right environment at the right time to ask for someone to do something for you. Debunk the theory that there is a place and time for everything and make the environment work in your favor.

For instance, if you are partying with a boss or coworker on a Friday night, instead of waiting until Monday morning to ask them for a favor, use the relaxed setting of a pub or bar. They'll be less guarded, more chilled out and relaxed, and in a more positive mood. Your chances of getting them to agree to the favor may be higher in a more relaxed setting where they don't expect you to ask for such a favor. Change the setting of where you'd normally ask something like this to increase your chances of getting people to agree.

Chapter 4:
Boost Communication Skills for Effective Manipulation

Manipulation is all about influencing people or getting them to do things your way. Thus, the manner in which you communicate certain ideas, thoughts, feelings, facts, and emotions are going to impact their decision.

Communication skills are vital when it comes to persuading people to do what you want them to without making them feel like they are being manipulated or pushed into something. Manipulation is a subtle art that can be mastered with the powerful verbal and nonverbal communication skills over a period of time.

Here are some of my best tips for improving your communication skills for manipulating or persuading people into doing what you want them to.

1. Be a People Reader and Analyzer

Every person possesses a distinct persona that requires a unique communication approach. Every individual won't respond to your manipulation techniques in a uniform manner. For example, instilling hesitation or self-doubt won't work with people who are more self-assured and self-confident.

Similarly, a person who is more emotional in their disposition won't respond favorably to logical arguments. Before you decide your manipulation strategy, listen carefully to other person's words and closely observe their actions.

Are they more thinking or feeling people? Do they take decisions primarily based on logic or emotions? Does their body language appear inhibited or confident? What is the best approach to move them into action? What are their strongest fears, needs, and motivators? When you gain awareness of all this simply by observing their words and behavior, there are greater chances of persuading them into taking the desired action.

Study a person's personality thoroughly before attempting to manipulate them.

Here are a few power-packed tips to enhance your people-reading skills.

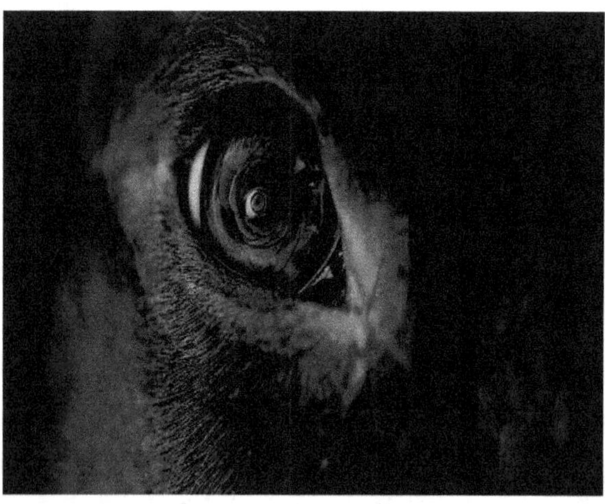

Analyze if people tend to give more emotional responses. These are the easiest psychological manipulation victims. Typically, they will cry during emotional scenes in movies/television, sob when their favorite character undergoes pain, feel drawn towards animals, feel an instant sense of empathy for the disadvantaged or underprivileged, and they are likely to treat other people's problems as their own. You can get these people to do what you want by leveraging their emotions.

Some people have a more rational approach towards arguments. They need empirical or verifiable evidence of what you are saying if you intend to get them to perform the desired action. You will have to deal with them in a calm, balanced and composed manner to rationalize with them since emotions won't generally move them. Usage of a subtle, balanced and gentle persuasion will work best on these folks.

2. Listen

Contrary to what people believe, communication isn't only about talking. It is as much (or even more) about listening to the other person.

The act of intently listening to people (put aside your phone and everything else if you want the other person to feel you are completely in sync with what they are saying) gives them the impression that they have your attention. From your perspective, you establish their personality and wants.

Listening to people equips you with the ability to come up with suitable responses to what they've just said.

For instance, if a potential buyer doesn't need a product right now because he/she is in the middle of considering another competitor product and you totally miss out on the part where he/she mentions the competitor product, you will only focus on why the need to buy the product now in your objection handling. Since you didn't even hear a bit about the competitor, you don't launch into a comparative analysis to establish how your product is superior or more value for money than the competitor.

Acknowledge what the person is saying by nodding in agreement or mirroring their expressions or making "hmmm" sounds. This way, the other person is encouraged to talk even more. Similarly, to make them feel like you are listening to them or to increase your understanding of what they are saying, simply paraphrase what they've said. "If I get you correctly Mrs. Rogers, you don't want to buy this product right now because you are looking at our competitors' features and prices too? Is that right?"

Don't interrupt the other person while they are speaking and resist the urge to offer your solutions before they finish speaking.

Even if you won't admit to it, all of us drift off after a point of time when another person is speaking unless you are absolutely captivated by what he or she is speaking. Asking queries and repeating the final few words after a person is a great way to clarify certain points or give them the impression that you are interested in what they are speaking.

Listen to the speaker with an open mind without feeling the need to constantly judge what he or she is saying. Effective listeners don't listen to judge their subjects or to reply. They listen to understand. Listen without concluding.

Again, avoid being a sentence grabber. Sometimes, people can't slow their thinking pace or mental capacity to listen to people more effectively. In such a scenario, they speed up and finish sentences for other people, when others are still in the middle of the sentence. I am sure you know one such person in your life that completes sentences even before you finish constructing it. This usually leads the hyperactive listener on a different trail of thought. If you frequently complete other people's sentences for them, you won't understand them. It feels as if you are having this conversation with yourself.

Allow your brain to create a mental visual or image of the communicated information. It can be a literal figure or an arrangement of concepts for the mind to stay focused with fully alert senses. Listen to extended stretches of conversation and always try to remember people's keywords and phrases. They contain a lot of information that can be used to manipulate them.

3. Body Language

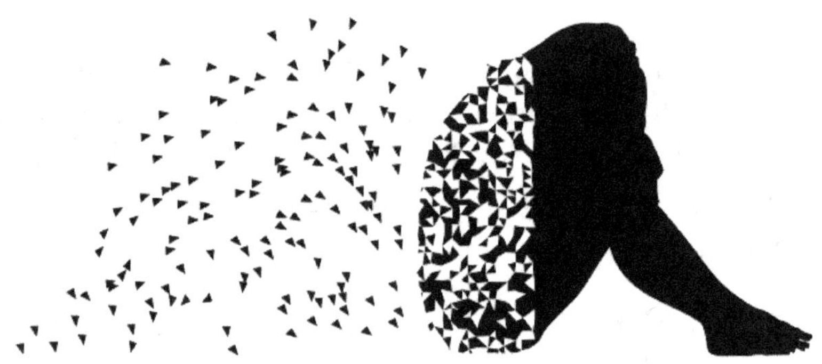

Body language is one of the most important aspects of nonverbal communication, which is why people always insist on having important meetings face-to-face when things can be easily organized over the phone or via an email. The impact of body language in the process of communication is vital.

Here are some of the things to keep in mind when you are using body language to manipulate people.

-People will be more taken in by the words and actions of a person who appears confident and self-assured. If your body language is sloppy, hesitant, and full of self-doubt, there's a slim chance people will buy what you are saying. Maintain an upright posture, avoid crossing your arms and legs, and keep a relaxed demeanor.

-Lean in the direction of the other person to reveal your interest in what they are saying. Your head should be slightly tilted in their direction without thrusting your face into them. Your feet should also be pointed in their direction. Don't get too close or you'll end up invading their private space, which is close them to anything more you'll want to say. However, slightly tilting your body in their direction or leaning over the tabletop is a good way to reveal your interest in them.

-While addressing the person, face them and look straight into their eyes. Try and maintain an eye contact throughout the interaction. Shifting away your focus every now and then makes you come across as an uncertain or dishonest person. Similarly, looking a person continuously in the eyes can be intimidating for him/her. It is alright to look away for a brief moment periodically.

-Be attentive and relaxed. Don't tap your hands or feet. Avoid fidgeting with your fingers or an object. It sends the message across that you aren't interested in what they are saying or are nervous in their presence. Leave your hands and legs in a relaxed position.

-A smile works wonders when it comes to striking a rapport with an individual on a subconscious level. Keep a smile plastered on your face while interacting with the other person to improve your likeability factor.

-One of the best ways for enhancing your body language communication is to practice in front of the mirror. It allows you to gauge how you appear in front of other people and what modifications you can make to come across as even more persuasive and influential to them. Closely observe your gestures, postures, expressions, words, tone, etc. as you speak. Is it capable of having the desired effect on a person? Do you come across as confident and convincing about what you are saying? Does your speech drive others into taking a quick action or does your speech inspire an instant action?

-Another technique for observing your body language, gestures, posture, leg movements, expression, walk, etc. is to record an important meeting or presentations. Each time you are in a situation where you are required to manipulate or persuade a person into taking an action, ensure that the interaction is recorded. This way, you'll have some reference material to fall back on when it comes to making the important changes in your manipulation-communication pattern.

You will know what works in your favor, and what you need to change to make your talks even more power-packed. I picked this up from a friend of mine who would record every presentation he would give to the potential investors and clients. He started with being really awkward and unsure. However, through careful observation of his body language and speech delivery, he could make the required changes. Over a period of time, he has become one of the most persuasive and influential communicators who can get people to do whatever he wants.

-When you meet a person for the first time (or any number of times), establish your subconscious authority with a firm, confident and assertive handshake. A limp handshake conveys nervousness or uncertainty, while a crushing handshake reveals aggressiveness or dominance. You don't want either of those. You want a handshake that's assertive and establishes your confidence/authority.

-Utilize power poses to your advantage. Amy Cuddy, a social psychologist, spoke about (TED Talks) how certain power poses help raise our testosterone levels and reduce the cortisol levels even in 2 minutes. These poses are known to have a significant impact on the way we think, feel, and act.

A majority of these poses involve making broader postures with your body that occupy more space and make your frame appear bigger. When you occupy greater space, you are subconsciously establishing yourself as a "larger" or "bigger" or "more powerful" person. While standing, widen your stance a bit by keeping your feet apart. You will come across as anxious or insecure if your feet are kept together too closely.

-Enhance your speech by using your hands. Brain imaging research has revealed that the brain's Broca region that plays a significant role in the speech production is stimulated not only when we are speaking but also when we are animatedly waving our hands. Speech and gesture are closely linked. Thus, by using our hands to gesticulate, we can facilitate our thoughts and words.

Notice how some of the best speakers will move their hands animatedly to make a powerful impact on the audience. You'll find your content improving significantly when you use gestures. Your thoughts will have more clarity and you'll utilize briefer, more impactful sentences.

-Watch people's feet to know if they are speaking the truth. When people who are aware of body language try to control their postures, gestures, and expressions, they often forget their feet. Since it is the least noticeable part of the human body, people don't pay too much attention to controlling feet movement.

People's foot movements will invariably increase when they are nervous, anxious, or stressed. Research has proved that you can determine a person's emotional state more effectively by looking at the entire body. When people are not speaking the truth, their toes will begin curling.

-To establish an instant rapport, align your body language with the other person. Face the person completely and directly to reveal you are focused on him/her. This is especially effective while communicating with a person within a group.

4. Tone of Voice

When you are about to make an important presentation or telephone call, let your voice relax into its maximum pitch. Keep your tone low and authoritative rather than high and squeaky. Your voice shouldn't end on the raised note at the end of a sentence. This simply signifies that you aren't sure of something you said or are asking a question rather than making a statement.

Allow what you said to end on a flat and assertive note as if you've pronounced a statement you're dead sure about. Personally, I love to use the authoritative arc, where my voice begins on a not, then raises its pitch in the middle of the sentence, and finally drops down towards the end. This way, you'll come across as more impactful and authoritative in your communication while manipulating people.

The tone of a person's voice can reveal a lot about how they are feeling. If the person isn't talking in a more even tone or there is a lack of consistency in their tone, they are most likely experiencing a surge of emotions such as anger, disappointment, nervousness, or excitement. You will need to look for other clues to determine the exact emotions.

Also, the words a person emphasizes on can reveal what he or she is thinking. For example, let us take a sentence like, "Did you borrow the bag?" Depending on which word they are emphasizing on, it will be clear what the person means. If he/she is emphasizing on borrow, it can mean she is asking you whether you borrowed the bag or stole it. Similarly, if he/she emphasizes on you, it can mean that he/she is trying to establish if you borrowed it or someone else did. If the emphasize is on the bag, he/she is wanting to know whether you borrowed the bag or something else.

Knowing what words the person is emphasizing on will throw greater clarity of what he/she is trying to communicate, which is vital from the perspective of getting them to take the desired action.

Animate your voice like a radio personality or your favorite voice-over artist. Don't speak in a monotone if you want to create the desired impact. Speaking in a standard tone rarely leaves behind a powerful impression. Raise and lower your pitch to create the required histrionics. Listen to radio presenters carefully to understand how they use the power of their voice to stir the right feelings in their listeners.

Again, the volume of your voice depends on the number of people you are addressing. If you are addressing a large audience, you may want to keep it louder. However, if it is a one-to-one interaction, speak softly and in a low volume.

5. Words

What words should you use to trigger people's hot buttons during verbal communication? "Hot words" are highly effective when it comes to influencing people by tapping into their subconscious mind. The human mind often links specific words/phrases with compelling emotions. There is deep psychological meaning attached to certain words and phrases, which means that they can be used for influencing the person to take a quick action.

Words and phrases such as "love," "genuine," "trust," "valid," and "assurance" evoke positive feelings in people. It creates a sense of warmth and assurance. People tend to react more favorably to these words.

Similarly, amplifying words and phrases that are spoken to elicit the desired response or create a desired feeling, much like hypnosis. You are simply hypnotizing people with your words. When you want to get a person to do what you want, use words and phrases such as "right now," "right away," "immediately," "quickly," "instantly," "suddenly," and other similar words. These words and phrases create a dramatic effect on the person's subconscious mind to trigger the required response.

Get rid of conversation fillers such as "umm" or "ahh" to make your speech more impactful. Cutting out these fillers from your talk or conversation makes you come across as more persuasive and forceful. Pause for effect when you make an important point. Let the significance of what you've said be absorbed by your audience. Verbal communication is as much about knowing when to pause as about what to say. Don't use words such as "like" or "really." These are unnecessary fillers that rob your speech of the desired impact.

One of the best ways to use words for manipulating people is to use the power of stories. Stories are brilliant when it comes to moving people into action. Stories trigger our brains in a persuasive manner by structuring a narrative into it. Thus, when stating boring facts and figures in a presentation form doesn't work, use the power of stories to influence, persuade, or manipulate people.

Speak loudly and slowly. Your words should be evenly spaced. Don't speak too fast or too slowly. Keep a moderate rate of speech. For maximum impact, speak in loud and clear voice while keeping your pace slightly slower than usual. Don't mumble or speak in an incoherent manner. It makes you come across as unsure and non-persuasive. If you notice people are asking you to repeat what you said every now and then, articulate yourself more clearly and loudly.

If you speak too fast, you'll come across as uncertain or nervous. If you speak too slowly, you'll come across as someone who gets stuck and needs help to finish their sentences. Hence, space out your speech more evenly.

Correct pronunciations are vital when you trying to manipulate people by establishing authority. People aren't going to take you seriously if you don't know how to say a word. If you are unsure about pronouncing a word, avoid using it. Learn at least three new words a day to use them to convey the right meaning during a presentation or interaction.

It becomes easier to manipulate or persuade people into doing something when you create the right impact by using the most appropriate expressions. Being articulate is significant from the manipulation point of view.

To make your arguments more persuasive, use simple, effective, and straightforward language.

Conclusion

Thanks for making it to the end of this book. I hope it was informative and provided you with all of the tools you need to understand the basics of manipulation and how it can be used in your everyday life to get what you want.

The next step is to simply use all the powerful strategies, tips, and techniques used in the book to control people's minds and persuade them into doing what you want them to without even realizing it.

The book is packed with actionable tips and real-life illustrations to help you develop a good understanding of the art of manipulation and how to use it effectively to get people to feel, think, and act the way you want them to.

Lastly, if you enjoyed this book, then I'd like to ask you for a favor; would you be kind enough to leave a review for this book on Amazon? It'd be highly appreciated!

Thank you and good luck!